DON'T TRIP OVER THE GARDEN HOSE
& Other Blood Sacrifices

DON'T TRIP OVER THE GARDEN HOSE

& Other Blood Sacrifices

Elsha Bohnert

DEUXMERS

Published by Deuxmers, LLC
PO Box 440, Waimanalo, Hawaii.

Copyright © 2013 Elsha Bohnert.
Cover painting "Night Monkeys & Ra" © 2013 Elsha Bohnert.
All images and self-portrait photograph © 2013 Elsha Bohnert.

"Motherless" and "Twenty-One Banyans" from *Traditions: A Tapestry of Time*,
originally published by Rain Bird 1998, Issue 19.

"Valentine" from *From Postcards to E-Mail: A Century of Messages*,
originally published by Rain Bird 1999 Millennium Issue 20.

"Birthing Stones at Kukaniloko" from *The Hawai'i Issue*,
originally published by Hawai'i Revue, Summer 1999, Issue 53, Volume 22.2.

"Collateral Damage" from *New Moon*,
first version published by Bamboo Ridge, number 75, Spring 1999.

"Lines" and "Rohatsu: First Koan" from *Light To See By*,
first version published by Loose Hair Press 1999.
Reprinted with permission of Loose Hair Press.

"Finding Grace" and "House of Gamma Rays" are printed
with permission from the linked poem collection, *Renshi/Albatross*.

"A bird that flies without wings is not necessarily a bird whose wings have been clipped."
is quoted from *A Little Course in Dreams*
with permission of the author, Robert Bosnak, M.D.

Artwork photographs courtesy of Marc Schechter.

ISBN: 978-0983504122

All rights reserved. No part of this book may be reproduced
in any form without written permission from the publisher.

Printed in the United States of America.

To the three wonders in my life: Monique, Phillip and Phil
And in memory of my mother Antoinette

CONTENTS

THE IMPULSE

SLIVER OF A MOON *12*
1946 PORTRAIT *14*
PICTURES I DIDN'T TAKE *16*
BIRD WITH NO WINGS *18*
SHOW AND TELL *20*
WAIKIKI LITTER *22*
TO THE GIRL WITH THE CHOCOLATE SKIN *24*
STILL BIRTH *25*
BIRTHING STONES AT KUKANILOKO *26*
TWENTY-ONE BANYANS *28*
THE KEY *29*
AUNTIE *30*
I THOUGHT IT WAS A GHOST *31*
NO IN-BETWEEN *32*
BEER AND BLOOD *33*
IF AIMED CORRECTLY *34*
COLLATERAL DAMAGE *35*

THE WOUNDING

MOTHERLESS *38*
STORY *40*
MAGICIAN *41*
KITCHEN FUNERAL *42*
LIPSTICK *44*
LIST *46*
GRIEVANCE *48*
SAFEKEEPING *50*
FUKUSHIMA 50 *51*
ALOHA OE *52*
VALENTINE *53*
HOUSE OF GAMMA RAYS *54*
BANSHEE *56*
PARK PLAY *57*
FLASHBACK *58*
TRANCE *60*
TOWER *62*
LINES *63*
BLUE FLAMES *64*
WHILE I KISS YOU *66*

PORTALS

    STEPPING FORWARD INTO THE PAST   *70*
    FINDING GRACE   *72*
    EVERYDAY FOOL   *74*
    ROHATSU: FIRST KOAN   *76*
    NOTHING HAS CHANGED   *78*
    WALKING MEDITATION   *79*
    RAZOR   *80*
    HOW THEY SAY I LOVE YOU   *81*
    I CAN SEE   *82*
    KARATE LESSON   *83*
    REMEMBER WHO YOU ARE   *84*
    ENOUGH TO DRIVE YOU CRAZY   *85*
    THE DILEMMA AT THE HEART OF THE STORY IS   *86*
    OH MY BELOVED   *87*
    WHY I WRITE   *88*
    I THINK OF DYING EVERY DAY   *90*
    SINGING   *91*

A bird that flies without wings is not necessarily a bird whose wings have been clipped. Perhaps it has always flown without wings, and this is just the specific quality of the bird.

-- Robert Bosnak, M.D.,
A Little Course in Dreams

THE IMPULSE

SLIVER OF A MOON

If I had lived
in that time of acute anxiety
in a country fractured
seething for blood

If I had been a girl sixteen
alone
unaware that her best friend –
who just got a brand new bike
and played boogie-woogie instead of scales –
would flee for her life
after a quick lunch of curry
her parents acting like
nothing special
just going for a short drive

If I had been the girl
threatened by soldiers
on her way to school
declared enemy of the state
banished to a land of winters
row houses
coalbins
potatoes not rice

If I had been that girl I would
have stopped and said goodbye
to geckos
liquid hearts of palm sugar
guardian banyan tree
fluted sighs of night monkeys
clutching watery dreams

I would cross and re-cross
the equator for nights to come
sliver of a moon
in a dislocated sky

1946 PORTRAIT

Moments ago she was little red
riding hood running through the forest
of sheets drying on the line
now she is perched high on a stool
in the chinese photographer's booth

skinny girl in sepia color
stopped in mid-movement
one hand reaching for the edge of the seat
the other tensed on her lap
feet not in sandals but strapped
into oversized shoes kicked forward
as if trying to jump out of the picture
and the depletion of war

her eyes
show the dread and longing of story
mothers grandmothers forests
shape-shifting wolves hunters
sewing stones into bellies
but look at her mouth

full lips
parted like a doorway
foreshadowing the woman to come
a night writer dreamer
spinning her lazy wheel of easy bets
and behind her
someone else

someone hard
sharp
up in an instant
precise
quick to draw blood
and rapture
from a tender and
dangerous world

little red wolf
in sepia colors

PICTURES I DIDN'T TAKE

Three tiny baby shirts
on a make-shift clothesline
strung between an aging bike
and an overflowing trash can.

A woman athlete in her nineties,
bent, blotched, wrinkled, barely
running but moving faster
than a walk, lips painted Salome-
luscious pomegranate red.

A little girl in a faded
pink-striped bathing suit,
salt-water-matted hair,
searching for feathers
among the grit and dirt
of browning banyan leaves
wind-strewn along the crowded
walk at Queen's Surf Beach.

She pauses to admire
her five bedraggled finds,
three common once-white
doves', two sullied black-
white mynah birds',

A vagrant's crown
clutched in both hands
raised high
in solitary triumph.

BIRD WITH NO WINGS

On my way to the ocean across the green
expanse of Kapiolani Park, I come upon
a brood of birds in a feeding frenzy:
twittering Japanese white-eyes to my left,
dapper little Java sparrows to my right.

When I edge closer, they flutter forward
as one, landing a few steps ahead of me
to continue their feeding undistracted,
determined to get the job done in spite
of my interruptions.

I do my best to be invisible, breathing
tiny wisps of air, muting my steps
to the rhythm of feed-flutter-feed
on my left, feed-flutter-feed on my right,
feeling the grass bend softly
under my feet.

Rude raucous mynah bird, missing
one leg, commandeers a path across
my careful weave of steps, demanding
complete and instant right of way
as if I'm just another willy-nilly bird to
push around, nothing but an old one
missing both wings.

SHOW AND TELL

This is my spine
each vertebra packs a library of arguments
to justify everything I've done
Here is my throat
red marks indicate levels of tension
don't confuse it with any kind of weakness

My shoulders are harnessed for work
even when there's nothing to do
My head is all hair and bone
My tongue remembers fantastic flavors
and wants them all back
And look how my chest comes to rest
on my sweet belly-lap
such furious tumble of holiness
and late-night fretting
My heart is made of rice but it thinks
it's nothing less than the finest of chocolate

I believe in fool's gold
I believe in not knowing what to say
I believe in getting off on the wrong foot

I offer my blood
my excellent corneas
liver and kidneys
as no-fault insurance
that we may learn to talk
with each other again

See these blemishes and irregularities?
They're part of my splendid design

WAIKIKI LITTER

Socks.
A flattened baby's sucker.
Rain-scumbled scrap of paper
with someone's phone number in blue.
Seven white feathers in a row on the sidewalk.
Who placed them there?
A lone match stick, its red phosphorus
head defiantly intact.

You can find all kinds of things, run over by cars,
left behind, shredded by the city's war-on-grass
mowing machines.

A whacked-open ball, insides exposed
like a perverted derelict flower.
A complete set of car and house keys?
Someone's got a problem.
A little boy's army camouflage sandal.
Brand new.
Mom going: "Now where did that go?
What did you do with it?"

At night a litter of homeless huddle
around the bus stops on Monsarrat Avenue,
under the bushes next to the zoo.
Tarps, tents, blankets dot the sidewalks,
a stone's throw away from where lions
and tigers sleep in cages, dry and secure.

In the morning,
Tai Chi in the park,
tourists in paradise.

TO THE GIRL WITH THE CHOCOLATE SKIN

kinky halo bushel of hair
a name like a prayer
who refuses to acknowledge differences
of ethnicities because we are one and because
we all come from Africa:

yes the moon shines everywhere and all clouds
come from the ocean but how can I love you
if you're not the other?
how else
can I reach beyond my own
pinched
everyday hungry self?

STILL BIRTH

Fish baby,
do you know your father?
He stands there, uncertain
on the dark edge of light,
shoulders turned away.

For you
the world remains sleeping.
Fragments of salt cake
drifting with the tide.

Your mother's ruby arms, valiant
rivers of blood
fail to warm you.
Her womb of liquid amethyst,
the only sea
you will ever know.

Swim, fish baby, show
a flicker,
one tiny emerald flash
of desire.
It will change
her fate.

BIRTHING STONES AT KUKANILOKO

The earth is red
where guardian stones anchor the womb.
A wild rooster,

like a neglected ancestor,
circles my offerings suspiciously, scratches
the dirt like an itch. Rice and roasted nuts

on ti leaves, slice of sweet bread, ginger lei.
Secret navel of O'ahu, where the wind
shakes my voice, labors

to drum back the name of every stone
as if it is not too late. Pineapples
squat in rows of endless duty.

The road is still not paved, but buses
will bring tourists here, the paper says.
Only the rooster cries. No lightning,

purple thunder, no more need
to push on thirsty rock with thirty six
young warriors watching, poised

to pledge their lives.
Where is the water now?
Above and everywhere

coconuts ripen, heaving
in the wind. They only hang
so long.

TWENTY-ONE BANYANS

Twenty-one banyans
planted at a time of great lawns,
etiquette, arrow shirts and white
mousseline gowns, four o'clock tea
served in the shade.

The walls are crumbling now,
but breezes still sweep through freely.

Near the end where the slope tilts
like a question, a phone booth
stands empty, blue plastic angles
at odds with the leisure of grass.

There is much to be grateful for
in this time of darkness:
hospitals laboring while the country
walks around asleep,
roots of banyans carrying messages
no phone booth can serve.

This much I know about dying:
it's simple, not always easy or right,
the faded school bus, wires running here
and there, the teacup already broken.

THE KEY

I'm living in a pinprick of a room
the fifth or third or seventh floor
of a hotel or maybe it's a school
stretched like a concrete ligament
over the sea of don't-look-now

I cannot find my key and wander down
slow-breathing hallways
dresser drawers piled with babies
reaching for their toes
a stage that leads into my parents' bedroom
and their unmade bed (don't look)

my mother is a hired help
scrubbing the floor on hands and knees
oh shit it's you
she sighs twisting her rag
you with the golden key

that's when I recognize its golden shimmer
above my head
way out of reach and any chance
for me to ruin us all

AUNTIE

I no do dis for fun
she says
eyebrows popping like jumping fish
one higher than the other

da tourists dey no care
she points at her two dusty bags
used and reused
bulging with plastic bottles
and soda cans
retrieved from the trash bins
along kalakaua avenue
on her daily walk
from the ala wai to her garden plot
at diamond head

one bus drivah he say
you no can ride my bus
coz you dirty

but I tell him
no
I clean
I doing dis for exercise

I THOUGHT IT WAS A GHOST

Awake at five
I stood at the window
bare feet sensing something strange
a sheet of white rose up and came to rest
on the waffled roof next door
rose up again and floated
out of sight

I didn't know it was my roof
didn't know my house was hit
by a tornado
impossible I said
not me
not here
I was sure it was a ghost

NO IN-BETWEEN

Is tiredness allowed in heaven?
would there be room for lying
faking things
breaking down
nose jobs
rattle-brain stupidities
that make each one of us so interesting?

My hairdresser in Kaimuki
hip archangel with scissors
will leave me ravishing
or wrecked
I may exit the salon
transfigured
in a glorified body
or not

Is heaven like that?
all or nothing

BEER AND BLOOD

When I was still the Center of the Universe
and people dared to make fun of me, I plucked
my son from the serpent of my brow, turned
him into a beast of shock and awe to rain
destruction until their streets ran red with blood.

It should have been a matter of days,
but in the end I got fed up.
Enough, my child, I called, *let's go.*
But he had grown a terrible taste for blood.
I should have known.

I ordered seven thousand jugs of beer
and pomegranate juice to stain it red like blood.
Cheap trick, I know, for luring him away.
It should have worked.
By then he couldn't tell the difference
between the beer and blood.

More years have passed than I can count
and still he's gone, wreaking destruction
in my name throughout the taunting universe.

IF AIMED CORRECTLY

Weapons of war used to be works of art.
Shields. Armor. Sword hilts.
No more.

Remember the hand-carved handles of aurora
blades inlaid with devil diamonds, malachite
and tourmaline? Or the gigasteel lance, forged

of mythril ore and reinforced rockbomb shards,
the emerald-studded halberd battle axe,
whips of dragon tails and multi-use claws

for shredding armored and formless foes alike,
peridot staffs and garnet wands for calling forth
the plagues and blinding storms of sand,

golden sickles, slumber fans, climaxe hammers,
black star boomerangs and glass-bejeweled nets
to put whole armies in topaz slumber.

My all-time favorite? The common needle,
truest work of art for disarming any foe
with a single prick, if aimed correctly.

COLLATERAL DAMAGE

Some things are meant to be broken,
targeted from great distance, smashed
without warning.

The air is thick with buddhas,
luminous, silent. I think nothing
of stepping right through them,
trampling beads, offerings
of flowers and rice.

Behind me an army of ghosts,
disgruntled ancestors pushing, quarreling,
glaring, pointing at empty bowls
    Where is our food?
merchants swathed in silk, white-powdered
concubines clasping their unraveling robes
(jewels, pearl-inlaid combs lost long since),
horse thieves, dirty-fingered peasants,
midwives, water dowsers, bedlam of lepers,
murderers, snake handlers, preachers, perfume
sellers, sailors, soldiers, stone throwers,
hordes and hordes of strangers fornicating,
spitting curses at the howling, ever circling dogs.

And all along
I think I act alone.

THE WOUNDING

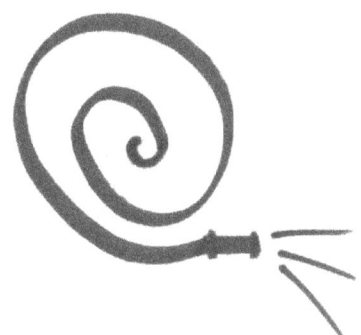

MOTHERLESS

My father flirts,
finds women eager
to jump in bed.
It drains my mother's blood.

The world
is full of such men
and mothers
who make themselves flat
and hard
and take a long
long time to die.
What do you do with grief so old?

I wish she would swallow a mountain of fire,
let lava pour through breasts, hips, legs,
pluck a thunderbolt from the sky, shout:

THAT'S IT.

YOU'RE DEAD.

I AM THE GODDESS.

I would throw back my head and laugh.
I would have found a mother.

STORY

I cry when he calls my name
come here he says right now
sit in my lap don't cry
I will tell you a story
a true story

I know his story
I know it by heart
I know how it ends
the puppy dies
because it does not obey
it dies again and again

He holds me tight on his lap
he makes dying puppy sounds
don't cry he warns
I can't stop crying
I don't want to die
he kisses me loves me
kisses me all over

MAGICIAN

Come
into my room
he said

I will change you
into a woman

KITCHEN FUNERAL

Strangers gather at your home for breakfast.
You breeze around your kitchen chipper as a
TV hostess setting out a perfect table but
really you've got nothing. The sink is stacked

with dirty dishes. You need to bathe, but
there's no bathroom and no time. Everybody
stands around in little clusters, whispering
about your failed uneven life, as if you're dead
and they are here for your funeral.

>   Quick, tell them you're sorry.
>   Call the police or something.

The chandelier is hung with unwashed
underwear. You need to pack your suitcase
but you're standing naked in the middle of
the kitchen with a man who is not your
daddy (but he could have been your daddy).

He's talking to you in a jelly-liquored birthday
voice.

Come here, he says.
Nice lips, nice legs.
You want it, don't you?
I can tell you do.

The words slide out the corner of his mouth,
like long hairs floating on thin waves of water.

You think it means he loves you. You think
you've found true love. He enters you with
sneaky finger snakes and giant elephant snakes
that make you want him all the time, as if
you're hollowed out and starving. The ceiling

buckles and your tongue feels like a stewed
tomato. Somebody sings a birthday song.
It's not for you. You're dead. You're dead
because you never said you're sorry,
because you never dared to say a word.

LIPSTICK

Look mama I'm a whore
you say I should not wear lipstick
this red
you're wrong
red is for laughing
smearing my name
on night mirrors

You never laughed but once
quickly turning your back
startled by your sudden spill
of crimson

I watch you pray mama
disinfecting your hands
your slender scripted heart
to be immaculate
for Jesus

but I
crave dirt
dark and moist
like an open mouth
and from your mute furious
backing away
I know
you wish that too
mama

LIST

don't
for-get
my teeth

she says
leashed to her rented
home-care oxygen tank

each syllable
an urgent whisper
but wait
there's more
two days away from death
she needs:

her roots done (one)
nails polished (two)
a perm (that's three)

a perm?
yes

teeth
roots
nails
perm

oh the beauty
of making lists
of things we think
we need

GRIEVANCE

Outside
a dappled ring of golden trees
shout out their buttery-yellow cries
of look-at-me hellos

Inside
bible in hand
death stalks my mother's bed
nothing to see here folks he jives
move on
jesus has washed away her sins

Outside
tethered to scaffolding and crane
I splatter every surface
wall and window
with words in spray-paint red
and roiling black:

She could have said I'm sorry
it's not your fault
I should have left him long ago
besides
he's not your father

Outside I say
she did her best
I'm not like her at all
and no
I never ever
think of her

SAFEKEEPING

My father and mother sit on a couch
Facing a large picture window
He on the right
She on the left
Chlorinated space in between

The light jack-knifes through the icy window
Silence rises from the floor like electric fog

This is how I keep them
Bloodless
Odorless
In cold storage

FUKUSHIMA 50

While we carry on as usual
nameless men in Fukushima
work and sleep deep in the belly
of the plutonium-spewing
Daiichi nuclear power plant
keeping it cool for years on end
their fragile suits and masks
no match for deathly rays
the steadfast beating of their hearts
our only hope

ALOHA OE

Shading my eyes I watch
her once strong silhouette
dissolve into the darkening waters
never stopping never turning
leaving behind a trail of petals
gentle ashes swirling
settling
into welcoming sands

VALENTINE

You never reached for me,
in the half-light of our marriage,
never wrote a message on the mirror,
window, papered wall.

That evening I was stopped for speeding,
my first ticket, but the cop saw my red dress
and waved me on.

Our house on northwest 31st street
had no sidewalk, no other place where you
could be a kid again, drawing your war
with chalk, your tanks, your guns,
your sky of lead.

You locked yourself in the garage
without a glance
at our crumpled cut-out paper hearts.

HOUSE OF GAMMA RAYS

My flight with feathers
silver words of sympathy
finger-touch suggestions
for music movies candlelight
can never be a match
for your determined barbed-
wire thoughts

we could be out with friends
instead you're locked inside your thick black
iron anvil suit and chains
unreachable

instead
I watch the slender needle
inside the meter
quiver its way from red-zone nine
to meltdown ten

shall I place a single coin
under your tongue?
payment for safe passage of your soul

cicadas
rasping fevered songs abruptly stop
why now?

I count my breaths
and feed the kids
in silence

BANSHEE

The way he tilts back in his chair
stiffens his lips and chin
veils his eyes
are clear signs to me
to back off
let my anger drain away
in slow even pulses

but I need
this rush of blood
pounding in my chest
salt scouring my eyes
anything
to break the metronome of rightness
expose the hiding places
kill everything that is correct and nice
and terrified

PARK PLAY

Kiawe trees spread their branches
over the old men playing bocce ball,
their hearty calls jostling the quiet.

Little boy in a red t-shirt
builds something with twigs,
body taut with concentration,
nothing matters, only this passionate
picking up and placing of twigs.
A tricycle sits parked nearby.

He doesn't notice his mother
gathering up the picnic basket,
big sister taking things to the trash,
father stowing chairs in the trunk,
looking up only when his tricycle
is carried away.
Crying, he skitters after it.
Father pays no attention, starts up the car.
The boy freezes in place.
Mother and sister, buckled up, don't look,
say nothing.

Kiawe trees lean in,
lower their branches.

FLASHBACK

Red-coifed cardinals
and singing thrushes feast
on berry-clustered trees. Tranquil

in the morning sun, pomelo ripen
big as cannon balls. Eucalyptus
gossip quietly among themselves.

A neighbor's phone rings
like a distant siren. A dog cries.
Hairpin curves slow down

the brown delivery van
searching for
the right address.

When airplane engines
shred the peaceful sky, I see
another tree, another time

when a child has stopped
to watch the silly feast of birds,
gone drunk on berries, ignorant

of coming doom, the deadly
curve of bombs.

TRANCE

I don't remember war only fire
sky of embers
lines of people shouting
passing buckets
someone pulling me away from the window

I don't understand war

A dusty road
prisoners being marched from camp to camp
women calling names of husbands sons
hoping for a sign of recognition
sun at noon a full catastrophe

Where there is no understanding
there is only trance
a continuous humming of the ancients

Riding my bike to school
I'm startled by a clatter of rocks
gauntlet of threats from people I don't recognize
why?
bloodlike spit of betel leaf
reminds me of my mother caught in crossfire
lifelong shrapnel in her legs

Over and over
I return to the humming of the ancients
soft drone of the earth in my ears

TOWER

I live
in a tower
with a thousand
steps and one
window away
from rain and
the shudder of storms.
A narrow stage for
narrow steps. Climbing
feels like going some-
here. Anywhere.
Anything can happen.
You can lose every-
thing even your coun-
try and be nobody. I
climb like a poem writ-
ten long ago, burdened
with questions. Child-
ren without names are
left by the side of the
road every day. They
don't cry anymore.
You can never pick up
all the pieces. It will
break your heart. Yes
it will even when you
stand tall like a tower.

LINES

I draw a line
it looks like a twig half-buried
like someone's crumpled fate
maybe mine

when your phone rang
you blew me a kiss
it's nothing you smiled
but then
rumors of war
cars vandalized
birds flinging themselves against windows
under wheels

and every day I draw a line
uneven scratches bundled in fours
to make five
in the end they hang like small
packets of grief
drying

BLUE FLAMES

In your faded coveralls
you start the lawnmower as usual
but all at once a strange blue flame
shoots out from you, not from outside
but from within.

You're fine but suddenly your mother
leaves without a note.
She won't come back, not even for
the holidays.

Her scented teak wood cabinet
becomes a coffin, then a boat.
You row it out to sea spreading
the lint and ash of rumors.
A storm hurls rain at you
the size of jewels, brindled beads
of questions.

Birds call from roof tops,
rocky shores, the grave yard
clinging to the mountain,
winter wildness in their cries.

What if years later you just happen
to round the corner, shoeless,
and come upon your mother
with her new and better family,
a worthy child?

Will you pretend you didn't see,
keep digging holes in ashen ground,
repeat your endless broken-wing routine?

Or will you step into your coveralls,
start up the waiting lawnmower,
let blue flames all at once
shoot out from you?

WHILE I KISS YOU

Tell me what you want he says
your wish is my command
whatever fancy frolic fantasy
I'll make it happen
group sex same sex interracial
doctor nurse sugar daddy
a little spanking maybe?
blindfolds silver chains
butt plugs feathers golden rain
I'm your slave
tell me what you want

    Really?
    What I want?

I want it all
I say
all
everything
and rape – especially rape
inflicted by me
be my father uncle stranger

and I will do to you
whatever I like
whatever
whenever
again and again
crucifixion yes
spear in the side yes
and not a peep from you
no cry
no sigh
no whimper
not even when I take a long time
to reach in
tear your heart to pieces
while I kiss you
love you
kiss you
kiss you
kiss you
all over

PORTALS

STEPPING FORWARD INTO THE PAST

I climb the steps between the undulating
dragon-snakes guarding the entrance
to the cremation ground
where fire leaves permanent shadows
and earth tremors scatter the ghosts

I give my name
maiden name married name place of birth
homage to my muddy river lineage of mothers
and grandmothers still at work beneath
the water grass and devil weed of history
I need them now

Kneeling I sift through ash with my left hand
for bits of bone a tooth stray coin
curled along the edge by heat
right hand steadying my heart

I was here once when I thought
I was dying and stood among the throngs
watching the spectacle of burning of the dead

Men sweating shouting heaving tall towers
of bamboo jostling them at intersections
bewildering the souls of the dead
to keep them from finding their way back

Intoxicating forward-backward clanging
of cymbals and gongs
merry mass of flower garlands
fluttering streamers
pungent odors of food and spices mingling
with sweat and incense
old priests with hair tied in topknots
flinging chickens into the crowd
squawking gifts from the gods

Maze of altars waiting for the sarcophagi
of mighty black paper-maché bulls
their bellies stuffed with a riot of offerings
and the freshly dug-up
hallowed bones of the dead

The flames triumph
smoke enters forgotten portals
and I take my place in the great hide-
and-seek swirl of mothers and daughters
stepping forward into the past

FINDING GRACE

We cling to life however we can
folding, refolding years of habit
scraping along the narrow sides
of this-is-it or maybe-not
But something has to change

I crouch beside my garden plot
a mess of nut grass, mites and centipedes
orgies of slugs, armies of unknown viruses
among my struggling kale and aging
collard greens

Heal, I say (as if it can be ordered)
Primordial lizard cocks his head

A sudden ruckus in the air
makes me look up in time
to see a gang of parrots – six
or seven – swoop overhead

screeching like doomsday prophets
warning of the end while racing
toward a vague horizon
in the hollow squander
bowl of sky

The silence when they're gone
tilts me into suspension
leaves me wondering what to do
with all the space inside me

EVERYDAY FOOL

One moment an earthquake
the next a tsunami
your bunker of knowledge breaks apart
twisted rebar in chunks of concrete
sweep past you
taking along your baby photos
diaries
DVDs
designer shoes

Throw your wallet after it
your brand new iPhone
hike up the mountain naked and young
someone asks for your arm?
give it
your leg? give it
you're a rose dropping your petals
with no thought

Next day the dogs of reality come at you
you rush out without breakfast
check yesterday's road kill of emails
more this
less that
delete
confirm
another war threatens
the rose has died
what's so important?

The earth will shake loose again
fires lurk in the wires inside your walls
and somewhere a cliff is waiting for you
to step off from as you follow
the fragrance of another fresh rose

ROHATSU: FIRST KOAN

On my knees
left foot over right
chest and chin just so
I try to sit like a don't-know
buddha

eight days of counting breaths
what is mu?
eight days of losing track
does a dog have mu?

nimble breeze tumbles
through the open window
damp with morning rain

right leg asleep
eyes half closed
I lock onto a spot on the floor
looks like a dog without a head

shama bird
swoops through the air
singing a no-thought song

makes me feel like nothing but
one big-headed dim-witted
wanna-be buddha dog
chewing on the bone of mu

all I want is to die peacefully
in my sleep

NOTHING HAS CHANGED

A whip of wind topples a sweetsop
tree onto the kiosk, straddling it
like an arthritic hobby-horse.
Last month's meeting minutes dangle
from a melancholy thumb tack.

Threats of revocation, arguments,
name calling, drugs, graffiti.
Somebody hacks off my kale,
rips out my neighbor's red-bejeweled
chili pepper plants. Cats drop
their litters under cherry bush,
bower of lilikoi, ginger patch,
contaminating the cultured dirt.
No end to grumbling and complaints.
Where is the peace?

But my body says: Cheer up.
All gardens are battlefields,
human sacrifice is still the norm,
don't throw away your clumsy
helmet and don't trip
over the garden hose.

WALKING MEDITATION

It may take a year to cross a room
or a half second to leap from continent
to continent
the pacific ocean fits
in your neighbor's lotus pond

women with hands like hummingbirds
weave your name into the cloth that hides
the holy mountain

don't ask for anything
don't turn from anything
just walk
follow your blind apple heart

take an hour to lift one foot
angels, lions, marys and jesuses
will rush to your side
you can't miss them

RAZOR

I watch him shave
while I wait by the shower door
for water to turn warm

bony shoulders over the sink
neck stretched toward the mirror
he guides his stock Gillette razor

through white cream foam
cutting perfect swaths
over cheekbone throat jaw

familiar time-worn face
an earthquake better not strike us now
breaking water pipes

crumbling walls
and both of us stark
naked past our prime

me shivering
he with his razor and his skin
so thin

so pale

HOW THEY SAY I LOVE YOU

He says
Don't worry about the dirty dishes
I'll just buy you another sink

She says
Thank you

He says
You haven't done anything
around the house for a while

She says
I'm doing the taxes

He says
You always have an excuse ready

She says
I learned that from you

He says
For me it's necessity

She says
I know

I CAN SEE

how much his spine
has torqued him to the left
bent his walk off-center
shrinking his steps
one pant leg lower than the other
support shoes worn uneven
the sidewalks turned into
hit-and-miss

yet his juju still runs fierce
shooting baskets with balled-up paper
making mischief on the stairs
his romeo wooing me singing
"funny valentine" off-key
stretching the line "you are my
fa-a-a-avorite work of art"

still
I can't help
but see the clutch
of fear when he looks up
after another fall

KARATE LESSON
In memory of Soke Kiyohisa Hirano

Bow
when you enter the dojo
when you enter anywhere
say *os* thank you

when you get hurt or sick
it's a good thing
bow
say *os* thank you

always pay attention
especially
when you're tired

so many people everywhere
but how many will be dead by next year?

make your mind so big
an airplane can fly in

then when you die
it will be the best thing that happens to you

say *os*
wow
thank you very much

REMEMBER WHO YOU ARE

If you want to be invisible
cover your skin with invisible eyes
If you want to fly

ask the seven sisters for milky way wings
When they wear out
ask the wind for a ride

Don't iron your clothes
and don't lose your accent
Remember who you are

The one who irks you most
is the one poking your blind spot
the one you asked for and need

If you want to rule the world
Forget who you are

ENOUGH TO DRIVE YOU CRAZY

I'm the one with welts
From purple fire DNA
Kali clawing burning scratching
How did she get inside?
I'm the one
Trying twenty-seven ways
To tame the fevered world
I'm the priestess of extreme
Inventor of the vinegar wheel
Inventor of the list of things to do
While staying in the Land of Benadryl
I am the sous-chef for the sultan of Brunei
The AK-27 avatar of crème brûlée
The potentate
The laughing stock
The weeping god
The monkey bar
The soul patch and the oscillating elephant
I am the fakir
I'm the basket
I'm the python in the writing chair

I'm fifty shades of fire
Scratching a path between what is
And cannot be

THE DILEMMA
AT THE HEART OF THE STORY IS

The pebble in the shoe
pea in the mattress
head in the sand
thorn in the side
eggs in one basket
and stepmothers of course
flying boys glass shoes
glass houses glass coffins
mirrors snakes blue beards
bloody keys absent fathers
mean fathers pussy-whipped fathers
frozen heart spaghetti heart
open heart surgery
and why would anyone build
their house with playing cards
and mark the path with bread
crumbs when you can wear
a crown of thorns at our everyday
banquet of plenty?

OH MY BELOVED

Furious dog lunging at my throat
submits to mad dog guarding it

    Oh my beloved

In the garden of lopsided coupling
I stumble, curse, nail myself to a rock

to keep from destroying the flowers
I tend and love

Eve in midlife crisis devours the snake
devouring its tail

New hearts are born and crippled
torn, sewn back together with threads

of parable and hope. The drunk
shouting obscenities is no other

than God singing , Oh my beloved
crowding out everything else

WHY I WRITE

Because I'm lonely
because the lines from me to what's

not me are tenuous or missing
and love has never been enough

because the puzzle is so puzzling
because I have no courage

no that's not it
because I'm told to look away

not think of the unthinkable
the catastrophe of drones and babies

who can sense it all but have no words
and those who don't or can't speak up

I must write with nail and claw
tarred head and splintered bone
burn my words to ash
break up the stone weighing
down my heart

oh who am I kidding?

palm trees stir with the chirps
of baby birds

roosters pump up their chests announcing
their moment-to-moment excellent mission

my good-natured plants though unwatered
remain full of faith and are quick to forgive

perhaps no one will have to die today

garbage trucks do what they do
nothing for me to figure out

everything I want is already here
everything written already lost

I THINK OF DYING EVERY DAY

In the garden
after digging and
loosening the dirt
I straighten up
set aside the tools
remove my gloves
and stand there
nothing on my mind

a car pauses at the stop sign
turns the corner and is gone

a sparrow fluffs its feathers
as I watch my feet
rise off the ground
effortless
higher and higher
becoming porous
all of me lifting upward
dissolving

nothing but city air

my ring drops
without a sound
into the gentle dirt

SINGING

When I was searching for my soul
the clouds gathered around the moon
the wind circled the earth
bringing the voices of children singing
oh why are you sitting on a stone crying
why are you covered in soot
dragging bags with petitions for love

When I was searching for light
the moon started shouting
the wind crept behind me
clear voice of my mother
rang over the ocean
oh why did you load
your bowl with stones
why did you cover the light of your birth
take back your impulse
your wounding
your portals

You know how to sing
your way home

ACKNOWLEDGEMENTS

Flower lei and chocolates to:

Shan Correa for firmly holding my feet to the fire.

Patrice Wilson for her generous heart and for introducing me to the amazing writing group of Carol Catanzariti, April Coloretti, Sue Cowing, Norma Gorst and Joan Perkins.

Memoir writers Kris Barry, Maja Clark, Sabra Feldstein, Victoria Gail-White, Jeanette Paulson Hereniko, Susan Killeen and Alice Anne Parker for sharing the journey.

Dreamstalker, Robert Bosnak, for introducing me to the alchemy and physicality of dreams.

Mark Travis, Kokopelli of Writing, for asking, "What would you write if you had no fear?" and for posing other irritating questions that make me cry and dig deeper.

And Phil, my Venusian husband, for being ever at my side and leaving corny love notes taped to floors, doors and the dishwasher.

Mahalo nui loa!

www.ingramcontent.com/pod-product-compliance
Lightning Source LLC
Chambersburg PA
CBHW071200090426
42736CB00012B/2393